THE LIBRARY
OF
ALEXANDRIA

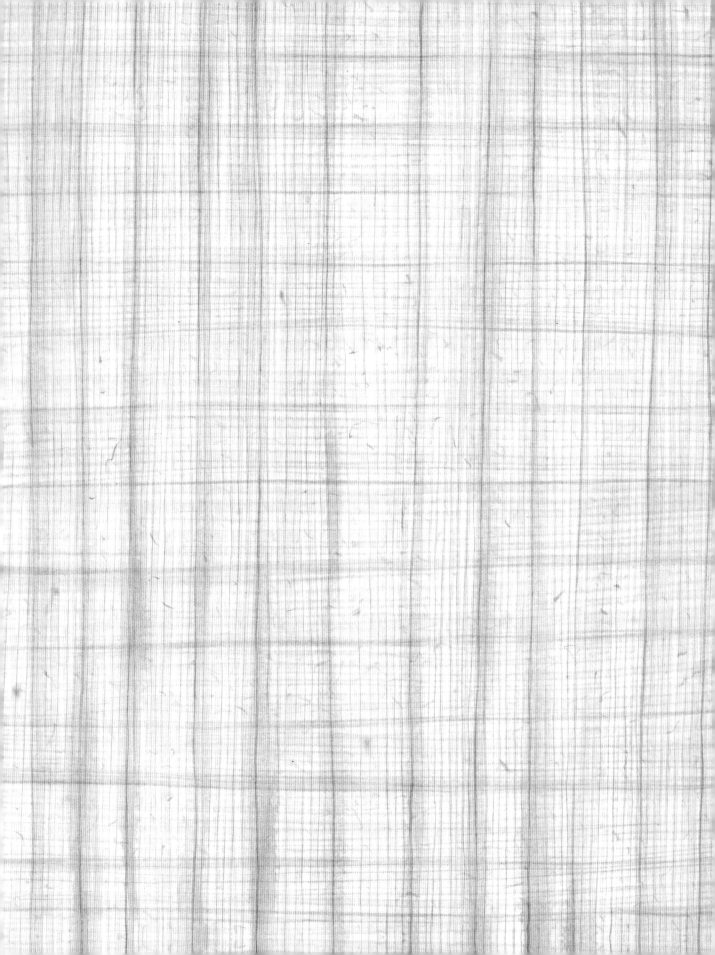

THE LIBRARY
OF
ALEXANDRIA

by Kelly Trumble

Illustrated by Robina MacIntyre Marshall

CLARION BOOKS / NEW YORK

Many thanks to Professor Farland H. Stanley Jr. of the University of Oklahoma Classics Department for reviewing the manuscript. Thanks also to the staff of the San Jose State University Library and the staff of the King County Library in Bellevue, Washington, for their help with my research.

Clarion Books
a Houghton Mifflin Company imprint
215 Park Avenue South, New York, NY 10003
Text copyright © 2003 by Kelly Trumble
Illustrations copyright © 2003 by Robina MacIntyre Marshall

The illustrations were executed in watercolor and gouache on Arches hot-pressed paper.
The text was set in 13.5-point Caslon Book.

Printed in China

www.houghtonmifflinbooks.com

Library of Congress Cataloging-in-Publication Data

Trumble, Kelly.
The Library of Alexandria / by Kelly Trumble ; illustrated by Robina MacIntyre Marshall.
p. cm.
Summary: An introduction to the largest and most famous library in the ancient world,
discussing its construction in Alexandria, Egypt, its vast collections, rivalry with the
Pergamum Library, famous scholars, and destruction by fire.
Includes bibliographical references and index.
ISBN 0-395-75832-7
1. Alexandrian Library—Juvenile literature. [1. Alexandrian Library.]
I. Marshall, Robina MacIntyre, ill. II. Title.
Z722.5.T783 2003
027.032—dc21   2003000150

SCP 10 9 8 7 6 5 4 3 2

CONTENTS

❧ I ❧

A CITY OF LEARNING

As ALEXANDER LAY SLEEPING ONE NIGHT, the Greek poet Homer appeared in his dreams and recited a verse:

> *Now, there is an island in the much-dashing sea,*
> *In front of Egypt; Pharos is what men call it.*

Alexander had wanted to build a great city in Egypt, and now he knew just where to do it. He immediately went to the island of Pharos. He ordered a city to be planned on the mainland, with a causeway connecting the city to the island. But the architects had no chalk for marking the lines of the city, so they used flour instead. Suddenly, an infinite number of birds rose like a great black cloud from the nearby waters. They swooped down and ate all the flour. Alexander was troubled by this omen. But the prophets told him the omen was a good one. It meant the city founded there by Alexander would be one of such abundance that men from many nations would flock to it.

This legend of the founding of the city of Alexandria has a grain of truth. Alexander the Great did indeed found Alexandria, and it did become a city of

The founding of Alexandria begins with an omen.

I

abundance: an abundance of books and learning opportunities, which attracted great scientists from many nations.

Alexander the Great was a Macedonian king who lived in the fourth century B.C. He conquered the great city-states of Greece, whose culture he admired. Then he conquered the lands from Greece to Egypt to India, spreading Greek culture and building the greatest empire yet known. Throughout his empire Alexander investigated the geography and founded many cities.

He saw the potential for a great city at the site of the Egyptian village of Rhakotis, on the coast of the Mediterranean Sea. A causeway between the new city and the island of Pharos would create two harbors. To the south of the city Lake Mareotis would provide fresh water and access to the Nile. The climate would be ideal for a harbor city. In 331 B.C., Alexander ordered the city of Alexandria to be built there.

But Alexander the Great never saw the Egyptian city that would bear his name. He died in 323 B.C., only thirty-three years old.

Alexander's empire was divided among his generals. Instead of ruling together, each general soon declared himself king of his own piece of the empire. The general Ptolemy became the king of Egypt. Ptolemy moved the capital from the old city of Memphis to the new city of Alexandria.

Ptolemy was a man who respected learning, especially in science. He decided to make Alexandria a great city of learning and culture. At its center would be the most famous library in the ancient world, the Library of Alexandria.

It was probably Ptolemy's adviser Demetrius of Phaleron who suggested that a great research center be built. Demetrius worked closely with Ptolemy to create the Mouseion, "the shrine of the Muses." In Greek mythology, the Muses were goddesses who gave inspiration to scientists, artists,

Alexander the Great (left) *fights the Persians.*

and philosophers. The Mouseion was also a great research center, similar to today's universities, that attracted learned men from many places.

Perhaps the scholars believed they needed the Muses for inspiration, but for their research they also needed a great library. So Ptolemy and Demetrius built the Library of Alexandria, near the Mouseion and Ptolemy's palace in the Brucheion, the royal quarter of the city, on the edge of the eastern harbor.

The Library of Alexandria was not the first library in the ancient world. For centuries the temples of Egypt had contained libraries of religious writings and records of events. Private libraries in the ancient world were owned by kings and by great men such as the Greek philosophers Plato and Aristotle. The first public library was in the Greek city of Athens.

But the Library of Alexandria was to become greater than any of these. The king owned it, and the scholars of the Mouseion used it for research under his patronage. Residents of Alexandria probably couldn't just walk in and ask for a book. Egyptians, who were treated as second-class residents under the Greek domination of Egypt, probably couldn't have read the Greek books anyway.

The Library continued to grow under the reign of Ptolemy's son and successor, Ptolemy II Philadelphus. But Demetrius wasn't in Alexandria to see his creation flourish. Before Ptolemy died he asked Demetrius for advice on which of his children should succeed him as king of Egypt: his children by his first wife, Eurydice, or his son by his second wife, Berenice. Demetrius chose the children of Eurydice. But Ptolemy didn't take his advice. He chose Philadelphus, his son by Berenice. When Philadelphus became king, he did not forgive Demetrius for the advice he had given his father. He had Demetrius arrested, and banished him from Alexandria.

Ptolemy and Demetrius observe the construction of the library.

2

COLLECTING BOOKS

TODAY NOTHING REMAINS of the Library of Alexandria. Archaeological excavations haven't given us any information on how the Library was organized, what the building was like, or even where it was. Our knowledge of the Library comes from books and letters that have survived the centuries. Some of these are whole, but some are just fragments.

Athenaeus, a writer in the second century A.D. who lived in Alexandria and did his research at the Library, wrote, "And concerning the number of books, the establishing of libraries, and the collection in the Hall of the Muses, why need I even speak, since they are in all men's memories?" The Library, along with the Mouseion associated with it, was so famous in his time that Athenaeus didn't even need to describe it to his readers. The reason for its fame was its collection of hundreds of thousands of valuable books. It was the largest library in the ancient world.

The Ptolemies yielded to no one in their efforts to collect books for the Library. Many books were bought in Athens and Rhodes, the main book markets at the time. But some books were acquired in unscrupulous ways.

Ptolemy III Euergetes, the son of Philadelphus, reigned in Alexandria from 246 to 221 B.C. He ordered men to search for books on all ships

Ptolemy III Euergetes' men search for books.

unloading cargo in Alexandria. Any book found on a ship was seized and copied. Because books were copied by hand, copies often contained mistakes, which meant that originals were more valuable than copies. So the owner didn't get the original book back. Instead, he was given the copy. The original was marked "from the ships" and added to the Library.

The original manuscripts of the great Greek poets Sophocles, Aeschylus, and Euripides ended up at the Library by another unscrupulous trick. These priceless manuscripts were preserved in the government archives in Athens. Euergetes persuaded the Athenians to let him borrow the manuscripts so that he could have copies made. For this privilege he deposited 15 talents, a huge amount of money, as security for their safe return. But Euergetes didn't return them. He sent the copies back to Athens and forfeited his deposit. The original manuscripts of the great Greek poets were added to the collection of the Library of Alexandria.

Although most of the books in the Library were Greek, the Ptolemies also collected books from many other cultures and had them translated into Greek. Manetho, an Egyptian priest, translated Egyptian records and wrote a history of Egypt in Greek. Hermippus, a writer who studied in Alexandria, wrote a book on the Persian religion Zoroastrianism that was probably included in the Library. Ptolemy II Philadelphus exchanged embassies with Asoka, the Buddhist ruler of India, so Buddhist writings were probably available, too. The Hebrew scriptures were translated into Greek for the benefit of the large Jewish community in Alexandria, and for the benefit of the Library.

During the reign of Euergetes, the number of books acquired for the Library grew so large that a second library had to be created. This was done at the temple of the god Serapis, called the Serapeum. This branch library was smaller than the main library, and is sometimes called the "daughter" of the first one.

Our best source of information on the number of books in the two libraries is the twelfth-century writer John Tzetzes, whose ancient sources of information are lost to us today. He wrote that there were 42,800 books in the Serapeum, and 400,000 "mixed" books and 90,000 "unmixed" books in

A scribe writes on a papyrus scroll.

the main library. A book was probably called "mixed" if it contained more than one work. An "unmixed" book probably contained a single work.

Our best estimate is that the Library of Alexandria, including the Serapeum, contained over half a million books. It was the largest and most famous library in the ancient world. But that didn't stop another ruler in another city from building a great center of learning to compete with the Ptolemies of Alexandria.

3
PERGAMUM

In ancient Egypt books were written on a material called papyrus. Papyrus was made from the papyrus reed, which grew at least six feet tall and was found only in the Nile Delta. The papyrus reed is now almost extinct in Egypt. But it was abundant in ancient times and was a valuable export.

The first step in making papyrus was to cut the papyrus reeds into strips. These strips were laid side by side in a single layer. Then another layer was laid on top of the first, with the top strips at right angles to the bottom strips. The strips of reed were pounded together until they were crushed into a sheet. Then the sheet of papyrus was smoothed out and left to dry.

To make a book, several sheets of papyrus were pasted together end to end. A wooden rod was attached to each end of the long piece of papyrus. Starting with the right side, the papyrus was rolled onto the rod to create a papyrus roll.

It was on these rolls that books were written. A scribe began to copy a book by unrolling a new papyrus roll a few inches, so that the writing surface was in front of him and the rolled-up portion was on his right. He wrote in

Making papyrus.

columns a few inches wide, unrolling more papyrus for each column. He used a pen made from a reed, with ink made of soot, gum, and water.

To read a book, the reader held the roll by the rods attached to each end. As he read, he unrolled the papyrus on the right and rolled up on the left rod the part of the book he had read. When he got to the end of the book, the papyrus was now rolled on the left rod instead of the right one. The reader had to unroll the book from the left rod and roll it back up on the right rod so that the next reader did not find a backward book.

A book made from papyrus had several disadvantages. Some books were on rolls 150 feet long, which made them a nuisance to unroll and then roll again. Eventually, text was written on shorter rolls—but a single book might consist of a dozen rolls or more. And papyrus was not durable. Each time a book was read, it could fray or tear. The ancient world needed a better way to preserve its literature, religious texts, and scholarly works. In the second century B.C. a better way was developed in the city of Pergamum.

Pergamum was a city in Asia Minor whose rulers wanted to make it a center of Greek culture and learning. In the early second century B.C., King Eumenes II built a great library in Pergamum to compete with the Library of Alexandria. His wealth and his zeal for collecting books rivaled those of the Ptolemies. Eventually, the Library of Pergamum contained 200,000 books.

To guard the reputation of the Library of Alexandria, and the reputation of the Ptolemies as the greatest patrons of science and scholarship, Ptolemy V Epiphanes found a way to cut off the supply of books to his rival in Pergamum. He stopped exporting papyrus.

Without papyrus, copies of books could not be made for the Library of Pergamum. But that didn't stop Eumenes II. He found a new kind of writing material, one that lasted longer and was easier to use than papyrus. This new material was made from animal skins. It was called parchment.

Writing on animal skins was not a new idea. But in Pergamum a new

Inside the Library of Alexandria.

13

technique was created to stretch and smooth the skins so that both sides could be written on. The skins of sheep and goats were used to make ordinary parchment. The skins of lambs, kids, and calves were used to make a particularly thin and smooth kind of parchment called vellum.

Papyrus had to be rolled, because it cracked when it was folded. But sheets of parchment could be folded and sewn together to form pages. A book made this way was called a codex. It was the ancestor of the bound books we have today.

The codex was more convenient than the papyrus roll. It was durable and compact. It could hold more text because both sides of each page could be written on. But parchment was also more expensive than papyrus, and several centuries passed before the use of the parchment codex became widespread. Eventually, parchment was replaced by paper, which was invented in China in the first century A.D. The use of paper to make books spread to the Arab lands by A.D. 800, and then across Europe in the twelfth century.

The rivalry between Alexandria and Pergamum went beyond competition for books for their great libraries. They also competed for scholars to use their libraries. One such scholar was Aristophanes, the Librarian in Alexandria in the early second century B.C. Ptolemy V Epiphanes learned that King Eumenes II was trying to get Aristophanes to move to Pergamum. Epiphanes couldn't let one of his top scholars defect to his rival. So he kept Aristophanes in Alexandria by putting him in prison, where he eventually died.

The Mouseion and the Library of Alexandria provided the resources scholars needed for doing research in many fields of study, including literary criticism, poetry, and grammar. But the greatest of these scholars, the ones we best remember today, were the scientists. Their work in Alexandria revolutionized humankind's understanding of the world. It was a revolution that would not be matched for almost two thousand years.

Making parchment from animal skins.

4

ASTRONOMY

ONE ASTRONOMER IN ALEXANDRIA is remembered today for proposing a theory of the universe that no one believed until eighteen centuries later. His name was Aristarchus. In the early third century B.C. he left the island of Samos to study in Alexandria.

The only one of Aristarchus' writings to survive today is called *On the Sizes and Distances of the Sun and Moon.* In this work Aristarchus assumes that the earth is in the center of the universe. The moon, sun, and planets rotate around the earth. So does the "celestial sphere," a sphere beyond the orbit of the farthest planet on which the stars are fixed. This is called the geocentric model of the universe, because the earth is at the center. It was the only accepted model of the universe in the classical world.

Aristarchus used this model to determine the relative sizes of the moon and the sun and their distances from the earth. The geometry he used was correct, but his measurements were inaccurate. He concluded that the distance between the earth and the sun was about 20 times as great as the distance between the earth and the moon. Today we know it is about 400 times as great. He also concluded that the diameter of the sun was

Aristarchus charts the stars.

about 7 times the diameter of the earth. Today we know it is more than 100 times as big.

Although his results were not accurate, they seem to have led him to an amazing conclusion. If the sun is so much bigger than the earth, doesn't it make sense to conclude that the earth revolves around the sun? Shouldn't the smaller body revolve around the larger?

So Aristarchus proposed a heliocentric model of the universe. In this model, the sun is at the center of the universe. The sun and the celestial sphere do not move. Instead, the earth revolves around the sun in a circular orbit, while also rotating on its own axis. Although we know today that the earth *does* revolve around the sun, no one before Aristarchus had dared to suggest that the earth was not the center of the universe.

No book by Aristarchus describing his heliocentric theory survives today. We know of it because it is mentioned in two books by other ancient authors.

We also know that the theory died soon after Aristarchus proposed it. The belief that the earth was the center of the universe was widespread and deeply felt. If the earth was not at the center of the universe, then humankind was not at the center of the universe, and that was unthinkable. The philosopher Cleanthes accused Aristarchus of impiety.

Later astronomers were interested in mathematical models of the universe, not just descriptions of what the universe might look like. The most famous of these astronomers after Aristarchus was Claudius Ptolemy. He lived in Alexandria in the second century A.D., when Egypt was a province of the Roman Empire. He was a Roman citizen, probably of Greek descent. He was not related to the royal Ptolemies.

Ptolemy's great book on astronomy survives today through an Arabic translation. It is called the *Almagest*, from the Arabic *al-majisti*, meaning

Cleanthes confronts Aristarchus.

"the greatest compilation." This book is filled with tables of astronomical data that allowed astronomers to calculate the positions of the sun, moon, and planets at any time. It also allowed astronomers to calculate when an eclipse would occur. The *Almagest* was the first book in history to provide a mathematical model of the universe that was good enough to match observations of the planets made with the naked eye.

But Claudius Ptolemy made one big mistake in his *Almagest*. He assumed, as did everyone else in his day, that the universe was geocentric. He created his tables of data starting with the idea that the earth was the center of the universe and the sun, moon, planets, and stars revolved around it. Because his calculations of the positions of the planets were so accurate, the geocentric model of the universe was accepted for many centuries. It became known as the Ptolemaic system.

Today we know that the planets revolve around the sun. A heliocentric model of planetary motion was first proposed in modern times by Nicolaus Copernicus in a book published in 1543. Until then, the Ptolemaic system had been accepted for fourteen centuries. Today, in spite of his great contributions to astronomy, Claudius Ptolemy is most remembered for having been proved wrong.

The heliocentric model of Copernicus in the sixteenth century sparked a revolution in astronomy. Eighteen centuries earlier the heliocentric model of Aristarchus was ignored. Today, after so many centuries, Aristarchus is most remembered for finally having been proved right.

Nicolaus Copernicus.

5

GEOGRAPHY

Duration of the reign of Ptolemy III Euergetes, the prestigious job of Librarian at the Library of Alexandria was held by a scholar named Eratosthenes. Eratosthenes was admired for his work in many fields, including mathematics, literary criticism, poetry, and philosophy. The wide range of his knowledge made him an ideal choice for Librarian. He was also the tutor of Euergetes' son.

Today Eratosthenes is best remembered for his work in geography. Alexander the Great's military campaigns had provided reports on the geography of new regions of the world, and these were available in the Library. Eratosthenes used them to draw a map of the known world, from Gibraltar to India, that was more accurate than any before it.

Eratosthenes' most amazing achievement was his measurement of the circumference of the earth. The circumference is a great circle around the widest part of the earth. The equator is one example. Another is a circle that goes from the North Pole to the South Pole and around to the North Pole again. Without modern technology such as satellites and radar, Eratosthenes came up with a measurement of the earth's circumference that was very close to correct.

Eratosthenes tutors Ptolemy III Euergetes' son.

Eratosthenes began his measurement by assuming that the cities of Syene (present-day Aswan) and Alexandria were located on the same longitude. He knew that at noon on the summer solstice a vertical pointer in Syene did not cast a shadow. On the same day and at the same time a vertical pointer in Alexandria *did* cast a shadow. Eratosthenes also knew that the earth was a sphere, and that the difference between the shadows at Syene and Alexandria had to be caused by the curvature of the earth's surface.

He estimated the angle of the shadow in Alexandria to be one-fiftieth of a circle. Then, by using geometry, Eratosthenes showed that the distance between Alexandria and Syene had to be one-fiftieth of a circle, too. This circle was the circumference of the earth.

The distance between Syene and Alexandria was estimated at 5,000 "stades." Because the cities were assumed to be on the same longitude, this distance also had to be one-fiftieth of the circumference of the earth. So Eratosthenes multiplied 5,000 stades by 50 to get 250,000 stades as the circumference of the earth.

We don't know exactly how long a stade was. One possible value makes Eratosthenes' calculation a little less than 29,000 miles. Another possible value makes it about 24,500 miles. The actual circumference of the earth through the poles is 24,860 miles.

In Eratosthenes' time, measuring long distances was far from an exact science. The number Eratosthenes used for the distance between Syene and Alexandria probably came from a traveler's estimate, not a precise measurement. Eratosthenes also assumed that the cities lay on the same longitude, but they did not. Alexandria was slightly west of Syene.

But Eratosthenes' method for calculating the circumference of the earth was correct. Even though his data were not precise, his calculation gave a result that was very close to the right answer. A more accurate measurement would not be made until the seventeenth century.

How Erastothenes determined the circumference of the earth.

Notes on the Circumference of the Earth

sun's rays

EARTH

a

stick at Alexandria
(shadow)

b

stick at Syene
(no shadow)

SUN

By holding up a circle to a stick driven into the ground at Alexandria and measuring the angle of the shadow cast by the stick at midday on the longest day of summer (a), Eratosthenes found that the angle was $1/50^{th}$ of the circle. Because he knew through his study of Euclid's *Elements* that this angle was the same as the angle from Alexandria to the center of the earth and back to Syene (b), Eratosthenes could conclude that the distance between the two towns was also 1/50th of a circle–that circle being the circumference of the earth. By multiplying the known distance from Alexandria to Syene by 50, he was able to determine the circumference of the earth.

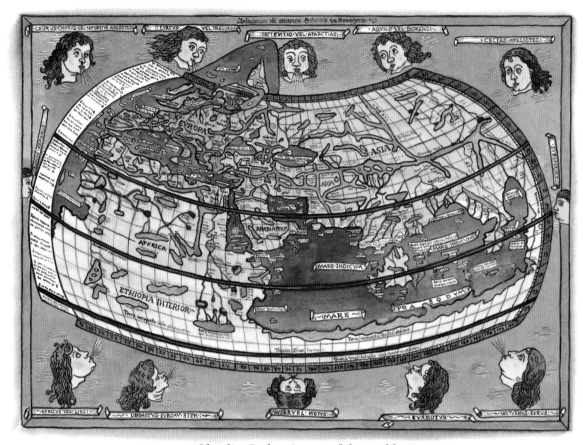

Claudius Ptolemy's map of the world.

By the second century A.D. Roman soldiers had marched into parts of the world that were far beyond Alexander's empire. They brought back with them new geographical data. It was time for a new map of the known world. Such a map was created by Claudius Ptolemy.

Ptolemy's map of the world was the best yet created. He used a system of latitude and longitude that had been devised by the geographer Hipparchus in the second century B.C. Ptolemy improved this system by accounting for the spherical shape of the earth. Instead of drawing the meridians of longitude as straight, parallel lines, Ptolemy drew them curved, as if they were sections of circles around a globe. In his book *Geography,* Ptolemy included his maps and tables of the latitudes and longitudes of cities and other places in the known world.

Ptolemy's map had many mistakes. He had to rely on the reports of travelers, and their distances and directions were only estimates. He connected Africa to southeast Asia, thereby enclosing the Indian Ocean. India was drawn much too small. But Ptolemy's biggest mistake was that he underestimated the size of the world.

Ptolemy rejected Eratosthenes' nearly correct calculation of the circumference of the earth. Instead, he believed the more popular estimate of about 18,000 miles. Since he divided the earth into 360 degrees of longitude, he calculated each degree to be 50 miles, instead of the correct 70 miles.

Ptolemy drew his prime meridian at the Canary Islands, on the far western edge of the known world. Then he mapped the world eastward, with every 50 miles equaling 1 degree. For example, if a traveler's report had put Alexandria 350 miles east of a particular spot, then Ptolemy would have mapped Alexandria 7 degrees eastward. If he had used Eratosthenes' circumference, he would have mapped Alexandria only 5 degrees eastward.

As he went farther east, these errors accumulated. By the time his map reached eastern China, the world between the Canary Islands and China stretched out through 180 degrees of longitude.

Today we know that this distance is actually about 130 degrees of longitude. Once again, Claudius Ptolemy made a big mistake. But these mistakes would change history.

In spite of all its problems, Ptolemy's map of the world was the best yet made. It was still the best in 1492, when Columbus sailed for the Indies. Ptolemy's small estimate of the size of the world and his eastern extension of Asia made the distance west from Europe to the Indies seem much smaller than it actually is. These mistakes opened the minds of Europeans to the belief that they had the capability to explore the world by sea.

New lands would be discovered, new maps would be drawn. And the European explorers would eventually correct Ptolemy's mistakes, the very mistakes that changed history by giving them the courage to sail the uncharted seas.

6

MATHEMATICS

The most famous mathematician of all time was one of the first scholars to move to Alexandria. His name was Euclid. He lived in Alexandria during the reign of Ptolemy I, and he died around 270 B.C. We know almost nothing else about his life, except that he was the author of one of the most influential books ever written.

Euclid is famous for writing a work on mathematics called the *Elements*. Very little of the mathematics in the *Elements* was his original work. Instead, Euclid rewrote all the knowledge of mathematics that had come before him. The thirteen books of the *Elements* show mathematics at its most elegant, with problems solved in concise, logical ways. Euclid's *Elements* is so well organized that it remained the standard geometry textbook until the twentieth century.

During his life in Alexandria, Euclid used his *Elements* to teach geometry to his royal patron, Ptolemy. It was said that Ptolemy asked Euclid if there were a shorter way to learn geometry than by using the *Elements*. Euclid reportedly replied, "There is no royal road to geometry." For more than two thousand years there was no better road to geometry, for royalty or schoolchildren, than Euclid's *Elements*.

Euclid teaches his patron, Ptolemy I.

Another great mathematician with ties to Alexandria was Archimedes. We know that Archimedes spent some time studying in Alexandria, but we don't know how long he was there. After his stay in Alexandria he returned home to Syracuse, from where he corresponded with his friends in Alexandria, including Eratosthenes.

In addition to being a brilliant mathematician, Archimedes was known in ancient times as an engineer. He explained how a lever can be used to move a large object with a small amount of force. An example of using a lever is when someone pries open a big crate with a small crowbar. The principle of the lever is so powerful that Archimedes is supposed to have said, "Give me a place to stand on, and I will move the world."

The Roman architect Vitruvius, who lived in the first century B.C., tells the story of a wreath given to Hieron II, the king of Syracuse. The goldsmith who crafted it said it was made of pure gold. Hieron asked Archimedes to find out if the wreath was really pure gold, or if it was an alloy of gold and silver. While Archimedes was pondering how to do this without damaging the wreath, he came upon a public bath. As he stepped into a full tub, he noticed that the volume of water that overflowed was the same as the volume of the part of his body that was submerged in the water. He realized then how to solve the problem of the wreath. He could submerge the wreath in water and measure its volume by measuring how much water overflowed. Then he could do the same thing with a lump of pure gold that weighed the same as the wreath. If the wreath was pure gold, then the amount of water that overflowed should be the same for the wreath and the lump of gold.

Archimedes was so excited by this discovery that he leaped out of the bath and ran home naked, shouting, "Eureka! Eureka!" *Eureka* is the Greek word that means "I've found it." Even today people sometimes say "Eureka!" when they discover something.

Eureka! Archimedes has discovered how to measure an object's volume.

Archimedes used his discovery to determine that the goldsmith had lied. The wreath was not pure gold.

Archimedes seems to have been most proud of his accomplishments as a mathematician. Many of his mathematical works still exist. In them he solved many problems in geometry, such as how to measure the area of a circle. In his book *On the Sphere and the Cylinder* Archimedes studied the question of a sphere that fits exactly inside a cylinder. He showed that the surface of the cylinder was one and a half times as big as the surface of the sphere. He also showed that the volume of the cylinder was one and a half times as big as the volume of the sphere. He must have thought that this discovery was his greatest achievement, because he asked that his tombstone be inscribed with a sphere inside a cylinder.

Archimedes was killed in 212 B.C. when the Romans attacked Syracuse. One story of his death says he was drawing a geometry problem in the sand when a Roman soldier approached him. Archimedes said to the soldier, "Don't disturb my circles." The Roman killed him on the spot.

In 75 B.C. the Roman statesman Cicero found Archimedes' tomb near Syracuse. The tombstone still bore the inscription of a sphere enclosed by a cylinder.

Archimedes defies the Roman soldier.

7
MEDICINE

Knowledge of medicine reached new heights in Alexandria because of the work of Herophilus of Chalcedon. We know that Herophilus was born in the Greek city of Chalcedon in Asia Minor and worked in Alexandria during the reigns of Ptolemy I Soter and Ptolemy II Philadelphus, but we don't know when or where he died. None of his own writings survive. We know about his work through the writings of Galen, a Greek physician who lived in the second century A.D., and others.

Many ancient physicians believed in treating patients by experimenting on each one with different therapies. They believed that the cure, not the cause of disease, was important. They followed the teachings of the great Greek physician Hippocrates, who lived in the fifth century B.C. and whose writings were in the Library of Alexandria.

But Herophilus believed that a physician must also understand how the human body works. So he became the first physician to do detailed research into human anatomy. To study human anatomy he needed a steady supply of human bodies.

The Egyptians probably didn't help Herophilus. Egyptians had strong religious beliefs about the preservation of the body after death. Embalmers

Herophilus examines a patient.

mummified corpses according to ancient Egyptian rites. It seems unlikely that they would allow a Greek doctor to participate in this process. It seems even more unlikely that they would deny one of their dead a proper mummification so that Herophilus could dissect the corpse.

But Herophilus did indeed dissect human bodies. We don't know how he got them. Perhaps some of them were stolen from graves. We do know that Herophilus lived at a time when Greeks generally did not feel the strict respect for the dead that their ancestors had felt. And so human dissection was possible.

There was one other way Herophilus may have studied human anatomy. The writings of other ancient authors state that Herophilus practiced human vivisection. That means he dissected human beings who were still alive.

The medical reason for human vivisection may have been that it was the only way to see the organs as they worked and the blood as it flowed. If Herophilus did practice vivisection, the unfortunate humans were criminals whom the Ptolemies handed over to him. But vivisection horrified most people. Tertullian, a second-century-A.D. theologian, called Herophilus "that butcher who cut up innumerable human beings so that he could study nature." Herophilus became famous for his knowledge of anatomy and infamous for the way he learned it.

Herophilus investigated much of human anatomy, especially the brain. He determined that the brain, not the heart, is the center of intelligence. His names for two sections of the brain are still used today in their Latin form: cerebrum and cerebellum. Even today a part of the skull, the torcular Herophili, is named after him.

Herophilus understood that the arteries carry blood. He was the first to count the pulse. He recognized the connection among the arteries, the

Herophilus and his assistants steal a body.

36

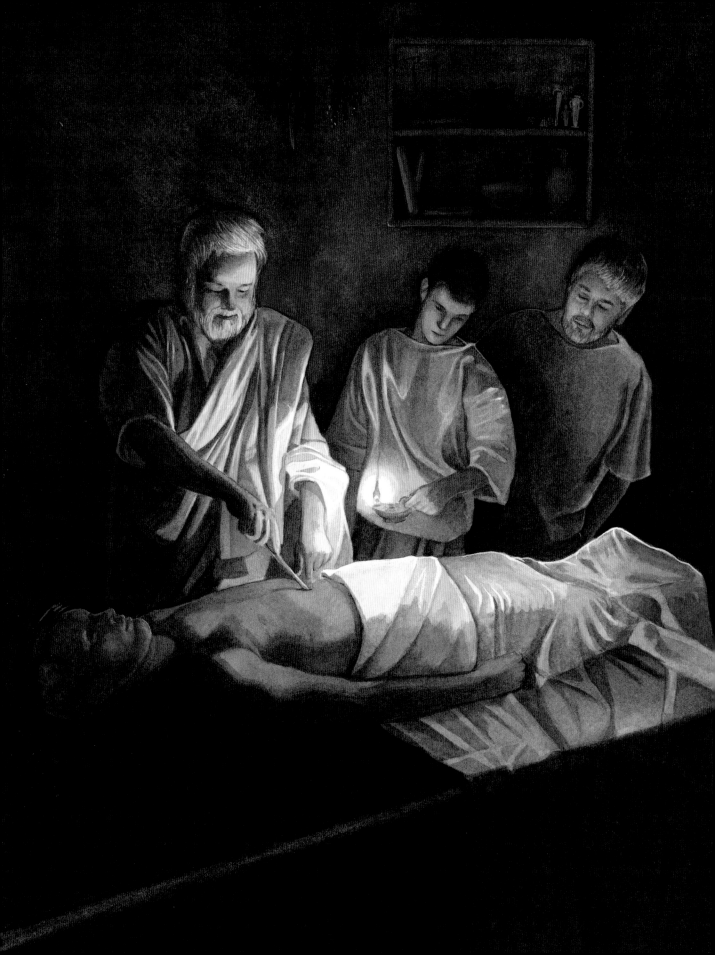

pulse, and the heart in a way no one had before, although an understanding of blood circulation would have to wait until William Harvey's work eighteen centuries later.

Herophilus also studied the eye, the liver, and the intestines. He measured a part of the small intestine to be the width of twelve fingers, so he named it the *dodekadaktylon,* Greek for "twelve finger widths." We know this part of the intestine today by the Latin form of the name, the duodenum.

Little is known of the physicians who studied in Alexandria after Herophilus. By the first century B.C. human dissection was probably not performed often. The religion of the Romans, whose empire was growing ever more powerful, and the religion of the large Jewish population in Alexandria would have disapproved. But around this time a skill for surgery was nurtured in Alexandrian physicians, a skill that could never have developed without the legacy of anatomical research left by Herophilus.

Herophilus begins a dissection.

8

DECLINE AND DESTRUCTION

THE REIGNS OF THE FIRST THREE PTOLEMIES in the third century B.C. were the glory days of the Library of Alexandria. The creation of the Library, the zeal for acquiring books, and the expansion of the Library into the Serapeum made Alexandria the greatest center of learning in the world. Great men of science and scholarship were attracted to the opportunities for research that only the Library of Alexandria provided.

But political chaos would ultimately destroy that which had brought greatness to Alexandria. Around 217 B.C., during the reign of Ptolemy IV Philopator, the Egyptian natives began a series of revolts against their Greek rulers. During the reign of Ptolemy V Epiphanes, Egypt lost most of its overseas territories to other Mediterranean empires. Then in 145 B.C., after a civil war with his brother, Ptolemy VIII Euergetes II became king and drove away the Alexandrian scholars because they had supported his brother. With this exodus of scholars, the Library of Alexandria began to decline in importance.

While Egypt was in decline, Rome was on the rise. By 49 B.C. the Roman Empire extended from modern-day Spain and France to Italy, Greece, and parts of Asia Minor and northern Africa. As the Roman Empire expanded around it, Egypt had little hope of remaining independent.

Egyptians revolt against their Greek rulers.

In 49 B.C. civil war broke out between the two rulers of the Roman Empire, Pompey and Julius Caesar. On January 10 Caesar crossed the Rubicon River, marching his troops from Gaul (modern-day France) into Italy, where Pompey was in power. He quickly overran Italy, but Pompey managed to escape to Greece. On August 9, 48 B.C., Caesar defeated Pompey's forces at Pharsalus. Pompey fled to Egypt, hoping to get a sympathetic welcome from Ptolemy XIII. But Ptolemy didn't want to be allied with the losing side. When Pompey arrived, he was assassinated by Ptolemy's agents.

Caesar followed Pompey to Egypt. When he arrived at Alexandria, he learned of Pompey's death. Caesar was no more welcome in Egypt than Pompey, out of fear he would annex Egypt to the Roman Empire. But he needed money to pay his troops. In 59 B.C. Ptolemy XII Auletes had bought Caesar's support for his right to the Egyptian throne by promising a huge sum of money, which he never paid. Now that Auletes was dead, Caesar wanted to collect what he was owed from the heirs to the throne, Ptolemy XIII and his sister Cleopatra.

But a civil war was raging between these joint rulers. Each wanted to rule Egypt alone. Ptolemy XIII had the Egyptian army. Cleopatra fled Egypt and raised her own army. They faced each other at Pelusium, on the east side of the Nile Delta.

With the two rulers gone, Caesar moved into the palace in Alexandria. His troops stood guard. Ptolemy XIII left Pelusium and returned to the palace. Caesar demanded that he disband his army. Ptolemy refused. He secretly ordered his army to march to Alexandria, where they would easily outnumber the few thousand troops brought by Caesar. Then their war with Cleopatra would continue.

But Cleopatra had other plans. She sneaked away from Pelusium and sailed to Alexandria. A friend rolled her in some carpets and carried her

Cleopatra arrives in Caesar's palace.

into the palace. The carpets were presented to Caesar and unrolled. Thus Caesar met Cleopatra.

Perhaps because of her charm and intelligence, perhaps because of her bravery in sneaking into enemy territory, Caesar took Cleopatra's side against her brother. Therefore, he was at war with Ptolemy XIII.

Caesar had sent for reinforcements, but they had not arrived by the time Ptolemy's army reached Alexandria. Caesar's troops held off the attack on the palace. But the Egyptians cut off the palace's fresh water supply. Ptolemy's fleet had control of the harbor, so no Roman reinforcements could get through. Caesar was trapped.

From this critical position Caesar made one of the decisions that made him one of the greatest generals of all time. He set fire to the Egyptian fleet.

Caesar thought this was a necessary military tactic. It destroyed the enemy's ships, so his own fleet controlled the harbor, and communication with his reinforcements in the Mediterranean was restored. But according to the Greek writer Plutarch, this tactic had unintended, tragic consequences.

First the fire burned the Egyptian fleet. Then the wind carried it to the docks and into Alexandria. The flames ran over the roofs, leaping from building to building. In their path, near the shore in the royal quarter, lay the great Library. The fire could not be stopped. The Library of Alexandria, the pride of the Ptolemies and the center of the city's intellectual life, went up in flames.

Soldiers watch the Egyptian fleet burn.

THE FATE OF THE LIBRARY OF ALEXANDRIA

THE ROYAL LIBRARY, which held hundreds of thousands of books, was now destroyed. But the daughter library in the Serapeum survived the devastation. Its collection of books was small compared to the collection held by its rival, the library of Pergamum.

Caesar and Cleopatra survived the war, but Ptolemy XIII did not. When Caesar's reinforcements arrived, his troops battled the Egyptians near the Nile Delta. Ptolemy XIII was defeated and drowned in the Nile. Caesar did not annex Egypt, but declared Cleopatra to be its queen.

Caesar was now the sole ruler of the Roman Empire. On March 15, 44 B.C., he was assassinated in the Senate in Rome. Control of the empire was soon shared by two men. Caesar's adopted son, Octavian, ruled the western half, including Rome. Caesar's friend Mark Antony took control of the east, where he allied himself with Cleopatra.

The city of Pergamum had joined the Roman Empire in 133 B.C. Now the city was under Antony's control. And so was its Library. Perhaps to

Mark Antony presents Cleopatra with the books from Pergamum.

make up for the burning of Alexandria's main library, Antony presented Cleopatra with the 200,000 books of the Library of Pergamum. It was the final victory for Alexandria over its intellectual rival.

With the books from Pergamum now housed in the Serapeum, learning continued in Alexandria. But there was much less scientific research than during the third century B.C., under the first three Ptolemies. Instead, philosophy and religion became important subjects for study. In the second century A.D., among the pagan temples of Alexandria, a school was created for the study of a new religion, Christianity.

Christianity quickly spread throughout the Roman Empire after the emperor Constantine converted in the early fourth century. In 379 another Christian, Theodosius, became the Roman emperor. He was a devout Christian who did not tolerate the cults and temples of paganism. In 391 he decreed that the temples of Alexandria be destroyed. The bishop of Alexandria, Theophilus, led a Christian mob to the Serapeum, the temple of the god Serapis. When he read aloud the emperor's decree, the mob went wild. They destroyed the pagan temple, and with it the last remnants of the Library of Alexandria.

The Library and the Mouseion, the pagan temple dedicated to the Muses, were gone. Alexandria became a center of Christianity, and remained so until the Arabs conquered Egypt in A.D. 642. They brought with them a new religion called Islam.

But the importance of the Library of Alexandria was not forgotten. In the thirteenth century a story began to circulate that the Library had been destroyed by the Arab general Amr. After his conquest of Egypt in the seventh century, Amr supposedly used the books of the Library to heat the baths in Alexandria. It was said that the books provided fuel for six months. We don't know why this story was created almost a millennium after the final destruction of the Library. But it was believed for many centuries.

A Christian mob threatens the Serapeum.

Today most scholars have discredited the story of the destruction of the Library by the Muslims. Some scholars believe the fire set by Julius Caesar accidentally burned books stored in warehouses by the docks, and that the books in the main Library were destroyed later in other invasions and by wear and tear over the years. But all agree that the Library's influence continued long after its destruction.

The Library of Alexandria, the pride of the Ptolemies and the greatest library in ancient times, is remembered as a catalyst for a giant leap in humankind's knowledge of the world. The scientific revolution that surrounded the Library was not matched for almost two thousand years. The Library of Alexandria is gone, but memories of the achievements it inspired live on.

A modern library (the reading room at the Old British Library).

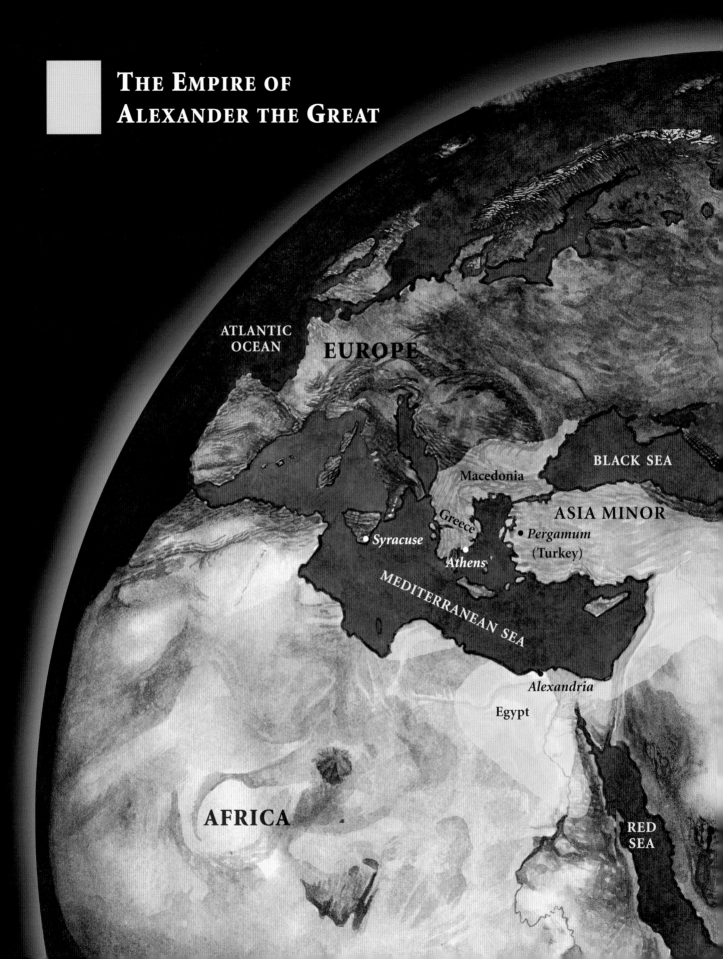

THE EMPIRE OF
ALEXANDER THE GREAT

ATLANTIC
OCEAN

EUROPE

BLACK SEA

Macedonia

ASIA MINOR

Greece

Pergamum
(Turkey)

Syracuse

Athens

MEDITERRANEAN SEA

Alexandria

Egypt

AFRICA

RED
SEA

ASIA

CASPIAN SEA

MIDDLE EAST

*Babylon
(capital of Alexander's empire)*

INDIA

PERSIAN
GULF

ARABIA

ARABIAN SEA

THE ROMAN EMPIRE
at its largest,
ca. A.D. 117

ATLANTIC
OCEAN

EUROPE

Britannia
(Britain)

Germany

Gaul
(France)

Hispania
(Spain)

Italy
• *Rome*

BLACK SEA

Greece

• *Pergamum*
(Turkey)

• *Syracuse*

Athens

MEDITERRANEAN SEA

Alexandria

Egypt

AFRICA

RED
SEA

ASIA

CASPIAN SEA

Persian Empire

MIDDLE EAST

ARABIA

PERSIAN
GULF

INDIA

ARABIAN SEA

PTOLEMY FAMILY TREE (PARTIAL)

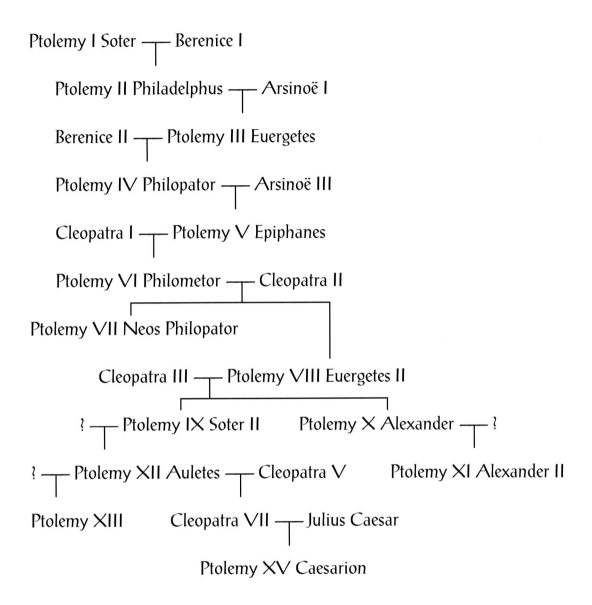

Ptolemy I Soter —┬— Berenice I

Ptolemy II Philadelphus —┬— Arsinoë I

Berenice II —┬— Ptolemy III Euergetes

Ptolemy IV Philopator —┬— Arsinoë III

Cleopatra I —┬— Ptolemy V Epiphanes

Ptolemy VI Philometor —┬— Cleopatra II

Ptolemy VII Neos Philopator

Cleopatra III —┬— Ptolemy VIII Euergetes II

? —┬— Ptolemy IX Soter II   Ptolemy X Alexander —┬— ?

? —┬— Ptolemy XII Auletes —┬— Cleopatra V   Ptolemy XI Alexander II

Ptolemy XIII   Cleopatra VII —┬— Julius Caesar

Ptolemy XV Caesarion

Portraits of Ptolemies on ancient coins.

SITES IN ANCIENT ALEXANDRIA

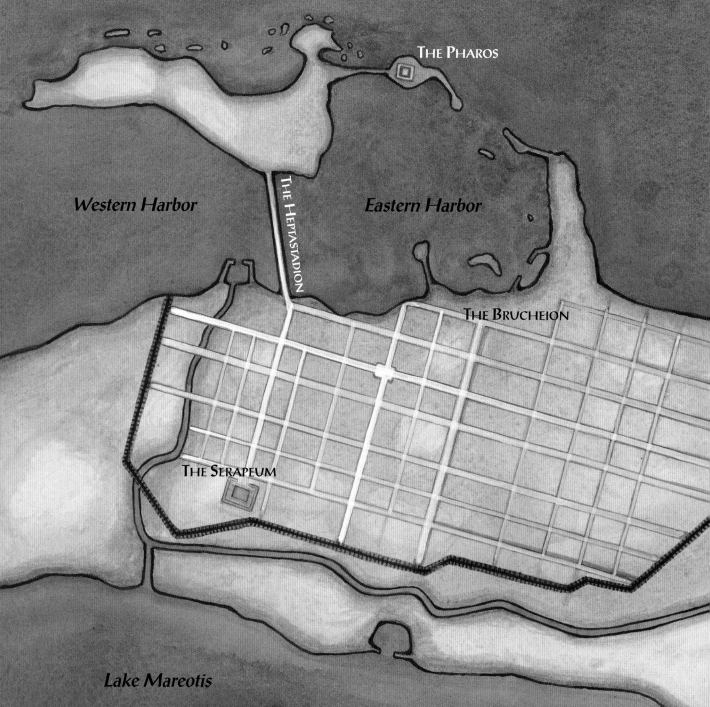

Mediterranean Sea

THE PHAROS

Western Harbor

THE HEPTASTADION

Eastern Harbor

THE BRUCHEION

THE SERAPEUM

Lake Mareotis

THE BRUCHEION

The Brucheion was the royal area of Alexandria. It was situated on the north side of the city, along the eastern harbor, and took up a quarter to a third of the city. In this area were the royal palaces, other royal buildings, the Library and the Mouseion, and various shrines and gardens built for the pleasure of the Ptolemies. In the third and fourth centuries A.D., military attacks and persecutions of Alexandrian citizens by Roman emperors destroyed much of the Brucheion.

THE SOMA

The Soma was the burial place of Alexander the Great and the Ptolemaic kings. After Alexander's death in Babylonia, Ptolemy I arranged to have the body stolen and brought to the great Egyptian city of Memphis. But according to legend, the priest at Memphis asked Ptolemy to take the body to Alexandria, fearing that wars would plague the city where the great conqueror's body lay. Alexander's body was buried in a tomb in Alexandria, probably in the center of the city. Because the ancient coastline of Alexandria has sunk so much over the centuries, the Soma is probably now under the sea. It has never been found.

THE SERAPEUM

This magnificent temple of Serapis stood high on top of an artificial hill in the southern part of the city. It was the home of the "daughter" Library, a statue of the god Serapis, and shrines to several other gods. The Serapeum was destroyed by a Christian mob in A.D. 391.

THE HEPTASTADION

The Heptastadion was the causeway between Alexandria and the island of Pharos. Its name comes from the fact that it was seven stades long. It was built early in Alexandria's history, probably by Ptolemy I. Besides linking Alexandria with Pharos, the Heptastadion created two harbors. It protected the eastern harbor, known as the Great Harbor, from the prevailing currents. But these currents caused so much silt to build up along the Heptastadion that Alexandria and Pharos were eventually connected by land. No part of the ancient Heptastadion has ever been discovered.

THE PHAROS

This great ancient lighthouse stood at the east end of the island of Pharos. Its construction began during the reign of Ptolemy I. It was probably paid for not by Ptolemy but by a wealthy courtier named Sostratus, who presented it as a gift to the city of Alexandria.

We know what the Pharos looked like because its image is shown on Roman coins minted in Alexandria. It was also described by several authors over the centuries. The Pharos was about 100 meters tall and built in three tiers. The first tier was square, and it tapered upward to a height of about 60 meters. The second tier was octagonal, and it stood about 30 meters tall. The third tier was cylindrical, about 10 meters tall, and on top of it stood a statue of the god Zeus Soter. A fire burned in the top tier and its light was projected out to sea, probably by using one or more mirrors.

The Pharos was one of the Seven Wonders of the World. Over the centuries it was damaged by earthquakes, and by the fourteenth century it was in ruins. Today the fort of Kait Bey stands on the site of the Pharos.

BIBLIOTHECA ALEXANDRINA

The ancient Library of Alexandria inspired the creation of the new Bibliotheca Alexandrina, inaugurated on October 16, 2002, by Egyptian President Hosni Mubarak. It includes rare books, manuscripts, a children's library, a library for the blind, and many other facilities open to scholars, researchers, and the public. The Bibliotheca Alexandrina was created in association with the United Nations Educational, Scientific and Cultural Organization (UNESCO). For more information, please see the Bibliotheca Alexandrina Web site at www.bibalex.gov.eg.

The Pharos at sunrise.

NAMES AND TERMS

Almagest (AL-muh-jest): Claudius Ptolemy's great work on astronomy, the first book to provide a mathematical model of the universe that matched naked-eye observations.

Antony (AN-tuh-nee), Mark (Latin name: Marcus Antonius): born 83 B.C., died 30 B.C. Roman general and ruler, friend of Julius Caesar, and lover of Cleopatra.

Archimedes (ar-kih-MEE-deez): born around 287 B.C., died 212 B.C. Syracusan mathematician and engineer.

Aristarchus (ar-is-TAR-kus): born around 310 B.C., died around 230 B.C. Greek astronomer who was the first to propose a heliocentric model of the universe.

Brucheion (broo-KI-on): the royal quarter of ancient Alexandria.

Caesar (SEE-zer), Julius: born 100 B.C., died 44 B.C. Roman general and dictator.

Cleopatra (klee-oh-PAT-ruh): born 69 B.C., died 30 B.C. Queen of Egypt and lover of Julius Caesar and Mark Antony.

codex (KO-deks): an ancient book made from sheets of parchment that were folded into pages and sewn together.

A girl reads a codex.

Epiphanes (eh-PIFF-uh-neez): "Illustrious" in Greek. Ptolemy V Epiphanes ruled Egypt from 205 to 180 B.C.

Eratosthenes (air-uh-TOSS-theh-neez): born around 275 B.C., died around 195 B.C. Greek scholar, geographer, and Librarian at Alexandria.

Euclid (YOO-klid): died around 270 B.C. Greek mathematician.

Euergetes (yoo-UR-jeh-teez): "Benefactor" in Greek. Ptolemy III Euergetes ruled Egypt from 246 to 221 B.C.

Eumenes (YOO-meh-neez) II: King of Pergamum, ruled from 197 to 160 or 159 B.C.

Herophilus (heh-ROFF-ih-lus): Greek anatomist in Alexandria around 300 B.C.

Mouseion (moo-SEE-on): a shrine to the Muses and a center of scholarly research in ancient Alexandria.

Octavian (ock-TAVE-ee-an): born 63 B.C., died A.D. 14. Adopted son of Julius Caesar and first Roman emperor, later known as Augustus Caesar.

papyrus (puh-PIE-rus): a reed that grew in the Nile Delta in ancient Egypt, and the writing material made from this reed.

parchment (PARCH-ment): a writing material made from the stretched and smoothed skins of sheep and goats.

Papyrus growing along the shores of the Nile.

Pergamum (PUR-guh-mum): a Greek city in Asia Minor that became a center of learning in the second century B.C.

Pharos (FAIR-os): an island off the coast of Alexandria, and the ancient lighthouse built there.

Philadelphus (FIL-uh-DEL-fuss): "Brother-loving" in Greek. Ptolemy II Philadelphus ruled Egypt from 283 to 246 B.C.

Philopator (fil-OP-uh-ter): "Loving his father" in Greek. Ptolemy IV Philopator ruled Egypt from 221 to 205 B.C.

Ptolemy (TAHL-uh-mee): a general under Alexander the Great who later ruled Egypt from 304 to 283/282 B.C. Also called Ptolemy I Soter ("Savior" in Greek).

Ptolemy, Claudius: born around A.D. 100, died around A.D. 170. Alexandrian astronomer and geographer.

Serapeum (suh-RAY-pee-um): the temple of the god Serapis, which housed some of the books of the Library of Alexandria.

Serapis (suh-RAY-pis): an ancient Egyptian god worshiped during the reigns of the Ptolemies.

A bust of Serapis.

SELECTED BIBLIOGRAPHY

Boorstin, Daniel J. *The Discoverers*. New York: Random House, 1983.

Bradford, Ernle. *Julius Caesar: The Pursuit of Power*. New York: William Morrow, 1984.

Clayton, Peter, and Martin Price, eds. *The Seven Wonders of the Ancient World*. London: Routledge, 1988.

Dijksterhuis, E. J. *Archimedes*. Translated by C. Dikshoorn. Princeton, N.J.: Princeton University, 1938.

El-Abbadi, Mostafa. *The Life and Fate of the Ancient Library of Alexandria*. Paris: United Nations Educational, Scientific and Cultural Organization, 1990.

Fraser, P. M. *Ptolemaic Alexandria*. Oxford, England: Oxford University Press, 1972.

Gibbon, Edward. *Decline and Fall of the Roman Empire*. London: Frederick Warne, 1870.

Gingerich, Owen. *The Eye of Heaven*. New York: American Institute of Physics, 1993.

Thompson, James Westfall. *Ancient Libraries*. Hamden, Conn.: Archon, 1962.

Thornton, John L. *The Chronology of Librarianship*. London: Grafton, 1941.

Tozer, H. F. *A History of Ancient Geography*. Cambridge, England: Cambridge University Press, 1935.

SUGGESTED READING

Ash, Maureen. *Alexander the Great*. Chicago: Children's, 1991.

Chrisp, Peter. *Alexander the Great*. New York: Dorling Kindersley Publishing, 2000.

Hoobler, Dorothy and Thomas. *Cleopatra*. New York: Chelsea House, 1988.

Ipsen, D. C. *Archimedes: Greatest Scientist of the Ancient World*. Hillside, N.J.: Enslow, 1988.

Knowlton, Jack. *Books and Libraries*. New York: HarperCollins, 1991.

Lasky, Kathryn. *The Librarian Who Measured the Earth*. Boston: Little, Brown, 1994.

Nardo, Don. *Ancient Alexandria*. Farmington Hills, Mich.: Gale Group, 2002.

Streissguth, Thomas. *Queen Cleopatra*. Minneapolis: Lerner Publishing Group, 1999.

Woods, Geraldine. *Science in Ancient Egypt*. New York: Franklin Watts, 1988.

INDEX

Note: Page numbers in **bold** type refer to illustrations.